CRANES

RYAN JAMES

A Crabtree Roots Book

Crabtree Publishing
crabtreebooks.com

School-to-Home Support for Caregivers and Teachers

This book helps children grow by letting them practice reading. Here are a few guiding questions to help the reader with building his or her comprehension skills. Possible answers appear here in red.

Before Reading:
- What do I think this book is about?
    - *I think this book is about how cranes work.*
    - *I think this book is about how cranes are made.*
- What do I want to learn about this topic?
    - *I want to learn what cranes do.*
    - *I want to learn the parts of a crane.*

During Reading:
- I wonder why…
    - *I wonder why some jobs need a crane.*
    - *I wonder why cranes are so tall.*
- What have I learned so far?
    - *I have learned that most cranes have an operator's cab.*
    - *I have learned that some cranes are yellow.*

After Reading:
- What details did I learn about this topic?
    - *I have learned that some cranes move supplies.*
    - *I have learned that all cranes have a mast.*
- Read the book again and look for the vocabulary words.
    - *I see the word **supplies** on page 8 and the word **mast** on page 10. The other vocabulary words are found on page 14.*

This is a **crane**.

Some cranes are yellow.

Most cranes have an **operator's cab**.

Some cranes move **supplies**.

How many cranes do you see?

Word List
Sight Words

a	have	see
all	how	some
an	is	this
are	many	yellow
do	most	you

Words to Know

crane

mast

operator's cab

supplies

29 Words

This is a **crane**.

Some cranes are yellow.

Most cranes have an **operator's cab**.

Some cranes move **supplies**.

All cranes have a **mast**.

How many cranes do you see?

Written by: Ryan James
Designed by: Rhea Wallace
Series Development: James Earley
Proofreader: Melissa Boyce
Educational Consultant: Marie Lemke M.Ed.

Photographs:
Shutterstock: Zoran Orcick: cover; Bjorn Heller: p. 1; OlegRi: p. 3; Dmitry Kalinovsky: p. 5; roundex: p. 7; Colorshadow: p. 9; Detailfoto: p. 10-11; Vladyslav Travel Photo: p. 13

Crabtree Publishing

crabtreebooks.com   800-387-7650
Copyright © 2025 Crabtree Publishing
All rights reserved. No part of this publication may be reproduced, stored in a retrieval system or be transmitted in any form or by any means, electronic, mechanical, photocopying, recording, or otherwise, without the prior written permission of Crabtree Publishing.

Printed in Canada/012024/CP20231127

Published in Canada
Crabtree Publishing
616 Welland Ave.
St. Catharines, Ontario
L2M 5V6

Published in the United States
Crabtree Publishing
347 Fifth Ave
Suite 1402-145
New York, NY 10016

Library and Archives Canada Cataloguing in Publication
Available at Library and Archives Canada

Library of Congress Cataloging-in-Publication Data
Available at the Library of Congress

Hardcover: 978-1-0398-3839-0
Paperback: 978-1-0398-3924-3
Ebook (pdf): 978-1-0398-4007-2
Epub: 978-1-0398-4079-9